A Duration

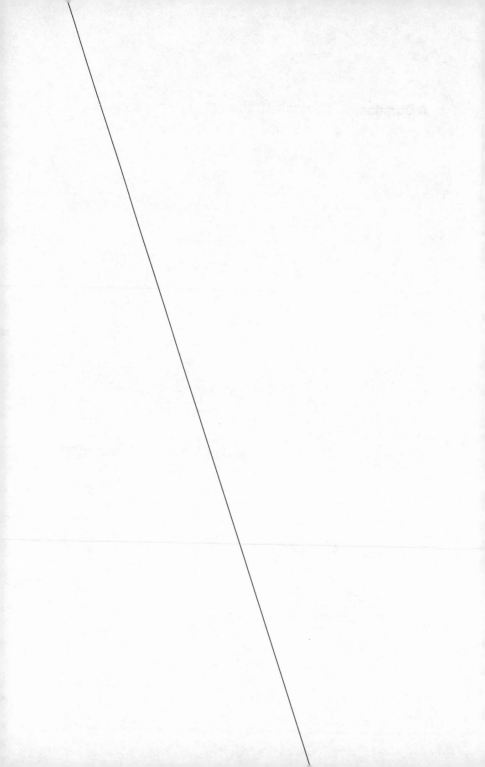

A Duration

Wave Books

Seattle/New York

Richard Meier

Published by Wave Books

www.wavepoetry.com

Copyright © 2023 by Richard Meier

Wave Books titles are distributed to the trade by

Consortium Book Sales and Distribution

Phone: 800-283-3572 / SAN 631-760X

Library of Congress Cataloging-in-Publication Data

Names: Meier, Richard, 1966– author.

Title: A duration / Richard Meier.

Description: First Edition. | Seattle : Wave Books, [2023]

Identifiers: LCCN 2022045042 | ISBN 9781950268788 (paperback)

Subjects: LCGFT: Poetry.

Classification: LCC PS3563.E3459 D87 2023 | DDC 811/.54—dc23/eng/20220926

LC record available at https://lccn.loc.gov/2022045042

Designed by Crisis

Printed in the United States of America

9 8 7 6 5 4 3 2 1

First Edition

Wave Books 109

Acting

She was imitating *The Great Gatsby*, the
part where a cloth is billowing on Daisy's
arms, by counting the words in each
sentence or naming the parts of speech,
and what she remembers is not what she
wrote but the sensation of the text

billowing and floating inside her a sound in
the knees a dust mote settling on the
blanket closing the right eye watching with
the left eye the left eye marking the pen in
its movements even as the right eye is open
the neighbor's flickering light and the car
going past and the groaning airplane sound
for a while. Scott studied how I

stood and sat, listened to how I described
the symptoms, and asked if I'd had
abdominal surgery. Yes. 45 years ago. The
scar tissues, he said, had bonded to the
layers of muscle, and the small pull ever
since had contorted the body. We lay on
our backs and as I struggle to say what
happened a large hawk or crow crashes

into the boxwood and a cloud of sparrows exits, a single sparrow, a sharp-shinned hawk flops out and staggers a few steps toward the house before flying off. Scott explained how we tuck the tailbone after trauma, that I'd never undone this, and suggested I release the six parts by imagining

the tail we no longer have dropping to the floor. How did that feel? It felt as if it were opening something in me that was closed and had been closed since I was four, yet I couldn't say whether anything had moved. I had tears in my eyes when I left and since then frequently have had the feeling of being released from a torment

I hadn't known was twisting me since I stood at the center of the sense that the oaks were spinning the first day I could walk again, the almost flat lawn had a steep slope, the fall leaves spiraling and making the sun flash in and out of sight, a feeling of

being submerged, of having been written
before by those older words, granted a new
idea, that being still him the possibility
remains of releasing what had been bound.
I have since been remembering my
searches for the scar, by sight in the decade
after the surgery when it was plainly
visible and then by touch through the years
the thickening hairs grew over it, curious
which side it was on

and if I could know. The orientation of
right and left, so long seemingly known in
the extremities, might never have reached
the interior, a sensation I had again
revealing it to Scott, pointing to the right
side of my shorts, checking for the scar in
my mind's eye while it switched from side
to side before sinking into place, as in
recent years I had not placed it on my body.
As I stood talking to him I felt I was
looking in the mirror, though I was not,
leaving me unsure if a reversal or
repetition would allow me to share it with

5

another person, the tears coming in part at
the thought

that my body had been left to suffer for
decades from this binding, but also by the
disorientation that divided or perhaps
doubled me. What needs to be accepted
right now is the question someone was
saying. The train horn blew, an airplane
appeared over the bridge, three pheasants
burst out of the primrose. It's nice to see
these things again and again. "Sometimes it
is as if the play has gone to rest up in the
flies; the actors have torn strips off it, the
ends of which for the sake of

the drama they hold or wind round their
bodies and only here and there a strip badly
torn off drags an actor aloft . . ." The earth,
rotating over my left shoulder, turned the
room more directly toward the sun, but at
the same time the sun was also turning in
galactic orbit, the motion hardly figuring
into the coming and going of the day, the
scar projected

onto the body, flat and distorted to a
degree one could navigate the sunlight in
the yellow folded wings of the grasshopper
where they join the thorax, black printed
on the yellow. The ice bell hanging from
the unseen was attached above that to a
tree limb, the ice growing around nothing
swung from the off-center tiny seed
matrix. Look, look,

a mouse! between the rows of Goldrush
wrote an *A*, a mouth-opening sound a
many-voiced open-throated singing with
hundreds, hills, carnival fire, happy
people, heathen countryside, forgetting
how brief how compressed, finding full
time joins by negating juridical being, heat
in the chest and outside in the form of

and the game Ferdyschenko suggests is
everyone say the worst thing they have
ever done—the Prince doesn't say, doesn't
have a chance to say—and I thought of
when I stopped and suddenly lifted James
off his bike after soccer practice when he

was six and shook him, angry and cold
after watching the practice, how could he
complain about not being allowed to stay in
the cold and wet to play on the
playground? And he cited this hurt years
later

when he qualified his statement that Rick
is the one who never hit or yelled at him,
that you never did but that one time you
did shake me and it was scary. I am very
sorry. Stein says, "going on . . . was at that
time the most profound need I had in
connection with writing." Today that is
painful. Hardly me,

the starling says. Turning to look it's Rick
walking with his cane dragging his foot
towards the office. A man in a car shouts
fucking pussy as I take a picture of the sky,
a fly on my hand, in my ear, John Clare's
paragraph addressing the fly as a friend,
and I realized I had imagined the last tenth
of the book as

the whole book and so hundreds of pages
in I have reached the long awaited
beginning, which also happens to be the
moment in the story when it arrives at its
composition, the composition of the
previous nine-tenths, the present of the
writing of the book, maybe all books of
this genre of the book being written,
though sometimes it is the beginning that
begins the experiment, I will have to look
again to see how it ends, a book in the
present, in which the whole is contained,
voices in a boot, people on their toes in a
boat, Judith overflowing like a pearl

What this means is it rhymes. A leaf floats
past underwater and studying it I see that
the procession of leaves is three-
dimensional, embedded in the surface and
depth of the river and the light is green in
the river water and yellow on the bottom.
The faces you see are there 80% of the
time, said agreeably, the stars shine all the
clearer when Lucifer has chased away the

brain shape, curled torso arms to elbows
spine soles of feet. The new fix-it guy who
lives in #3

told me Rick is in the hospital with liver
troubles. "He was going to come home, but
they keep finding new things." Home is #7.
I'd felt his absence, asked his last name,
Abele, so I can see him in the hospital. One
of the rules is not to look at things

before they happen and not to see them or
write them down before they happen not
to call them into existence by seeing or
looking or thinking or writing things
before they happen

not so they won't happen or won't happen
more or less or always before and after and
also in many places at once

but to conceive inside and out, to take in
absorb catch, to become pregnant with and
by, to produce generate contain hold, to
perceive, to catch, to form an idea of, to

imagine devise undertake, to pronounce
solemnly, to utter, to take to declare, to
express in formal language. A stone-
cutting saw has been whining and
grinding. The yellow butterfly

flaps hard over the maple 80 feet up then
drifts down, because things can be seen
from so far off. Creeping thistle scrapes my
leg, tiny purple-and-yellow asters grow
through the banister, white sock from the
line drops into the gravel. A child on the
swing down there disappears behind

a tree and reappears on the other side. The
hurricane has passed and the debt collector
quietly arrives. I brought a milkweed pod
in the house and someone said it was like
the scales of a fish, the seeds folded inside,
it was a fish most

fish-like, and we admired the golden spiral
in the brown seeds and felt the shiny glossy
feathery smoothness. Outside I strewed
them on the hood to mark their departure

and as they pulled away James rolled down
the window and shouted Mom

thinks a milkweed seed is definitely an
animal. I dragged the dragon, elk, or
horse's head in the form of a cottonwood
root architecture a mile through the sand,
arms reaching behind me like the traces on
a donkey, leaving a trail of 20- or 30- or
40-step segments after each of which I
stopped exhausted and leaned back against
the structure, propping it up as it propped
up me, looking back over my right shoulder
at still only the barest crescent of the moon
until

I caught my breath and began the next,
intending to continue straight but always,
as each subsequent look over my shoulder
showed me, zigging or zagging from my
intended route, each return to the path a
deviation from it. After I told the story, I
made wild motions while saying, See, a
companion approaches. Maggie said yes
the mood that would be lifted by beginning
prevented

beginning but beginning with the objects of the mood—phone case was dirty and needed to be cleaned, my room had a funk to it and maybe I should burn a candle—transformed those things into parts of a world. My toe went through the speck of glitter as I descended the stairs. Ryen said in the time she kept a daily journal doing so made space for it and on a day she skipped the whole day was off-kilter. "I recorded things that couldn't make any difference,

I had pound cake for breakfast or the impression I formed of a person the first time I spoke to them and everything they opened up to me about in our first meeting." The letters of the words must be written in an order that corresponds and when the thoughts lag, the words lag, the letter of a subsequent word appears, a future. The looped root on the concrete pad teaches

the loops are closed below the ground, but it was the lake action that unearthed it, removed the bark and soil, and cast it

ashore intact with parts torn and rotted.
The dragging brought it close, the letters
put something here. The muskrats have
been activated by the warming or
something else. I note one wake's black V
has no one at the head, the creature that
made it having died or otherwise
disappeared into the depths. *Dived* I meant
to write, but the letter at the center can
also leave

that feeling of really being known. What
gives you that feeling? Rick in the hospital
had a very light beard, the light of the
room shone sideways through it, as the sun
through the squirrel's ear a month later,
and seemed peaceful. The whole time we
talked, ten minutes, he had the TV remote
with a speaker built into it that played the
sound on his chest and his eyes flicked back
and forth between me and

the screen. His hand, as when he'd taken
mine before, was dry and warm. He said it
was good to know someone was worrying
about him, thinking about him, and that he

planned to be back at the Beach Aire soon.
He had blood clots in both legs, he said, but
the right is clear now. He showed me its
movement where the foot came out from
under the sheet. The left is still blocked.
Afterwards I walked at the south unit of
Illinois Beach State Park

and a group of four diver ducks, brownish
blue with pointed feathers, dove under. I
walked up the beach to the power plant and
picked up four pebbles. At the fence a
small stream, hardly moving in the long
grass, raced over others, thousands more,
where it had cut a narrow bed in the sand.
Small oaks with perfect crowns, each one
shifted as I approached, stretching to
twice my height while the trunk narrowed
to less than

the circumference of one of my thin legs,
the one I balanced on at the moment they
came forward. A fire burned beside one of
the five or six RVs. There was no one in
sight and I smell the smoke again as I read

the asphalt broken or
bending down softly

a vibration inside the thigh
muscle

on successive scraps of paper. A seagull
dove into the water and surfaced with
nothing in its mouth. Little biting pin
songs lingered, somatic songs linked
between bodies

grounded by yesterday's patterns
breathing through the soles of the feet,
the light shining through from the back
compressing the flowers. The red path
around the center of the pebble moves up
and down. The pebbles on the table are a
family and I love them including the ones
left in the pebble bank by the lake as the
tension repeatedly stored releases

the mulberry flesh between bark and
branch the squirrel eats then hops with an
acorn through a leaf. Gena Rowlands in
Opening Night talks to the dead girl in the
bathroom and admits she sees her but it's
not what they think. She made her up
because she wanted to know her. Watching
the end, the scene I've been unable to
reach for 20 years for fear of what precedes

it, included the thumb saying get out
and the escalating unhappiness inside
happiness I recognized from a scene I'd
just done in a staging of skits from *Your
Show of Shows*, our cast a motley of
children and adults. "Are you the ghost?"
we said to each other. "You think I'm a
ghost because you think you know me,
because you think I didn't get you a
birthday present. But you don't know me.
I know you." The living originals remained
backstage, out front, in the wings. I
listened in fear, then joy, as the people
grew to life scale. I thought of picturing,

while reading a poem, not images in the
poem, but a person writing, perhaps in a
way or place the poem indicates, with
those words somehow having come to that
place where a person is writing

another person

a pencil shaving or tiny browning blossom
or part of the skin of a peanut

the crumpled edge removed from a page
torn from a spiral notebook crumpled and
resting on a thin end and thick end so the
middle is raised off the floor so it seems to
be a creature. F. said, on hearing a version
of this, she'd read to her class the day
before

a poem of hers she'd translated from
Swedish back into English, producing a
version that responded both to the
unknown tongue and the known poem,
including the lines "he was her favorite
boat / he mothered her." Lying on the floor
words, perhaps these, had formed and
dissolved, formed again, each time
replaced by the bodily sensations, a
tightness

in the skin around the skull, the lips
gripping the teeth and releasing them, the
sudden slide of a gravel bank on either side
of me, landslides that had begun with the
trickles of sand grains, then pebbles, and
culminated, as I stood transfixed, in the
collapse of a section

of the low bank days earlier. The sand in
clouds and the pebbles in slow hops were
swept by the current toward the lake, my
torso in the river's place, and the collapsing
banks in the place of my arms. As the pain
in my left shoulder intensified, burning and
tingling for the duration of not moving,
though it is difficult to say, cut off in that
way, how much time has passed in any
given state, equilateral pyramids extending
out in all directions, wave sounds
increasing, the moss in the valley of

the bark? The first time we watched *A
Midsummer Night's Dream*, Helena and
Hermia made out for like three seconds, a
boy says walking past. Spenser has
arranged the moments

of anticipation, intense pleasure, and rest
in intervals that follow the golden ratio,
Maria said, believing the human body
functions in that rhythm, and so will be in
harmony with the book and so the
movements of the book are already in the
reader and the movements of the reader are

already in the book, and the rhythms of
reading become the subject of the book,
where the reader learns them and confirms

their truth. The sun came through a hole in
the forest where last night we'd walked
east to find moon holes,

and the moon and the sun in an instant
changed places. The wind lifted the tent
from the ground and it floated on the guy
wires. It was when Kozintsev said a new
project wells and surges to a new living and
the particular world however small and
distant brings forth the further one goes in
a greater and greater realism

the motions on the page seemed to be
moving backwards, the words appearing at
the sentence end flying back to the start.
There's no sun but behind the clouds and
the squirrel's ears are glowing white as it
turns and chews and turns a nut. What did
I fear in not watching the end of *Opening
Night*,

the failure on stage? Max asked. No I
feared the death of the imagined girl so
much I hadn't remembered it or known
until I wrote this it was the violence
between vision and visionary I feared to be
so bereft, as drunk as a person can be in the
fear I couldn't walk out on the stage and
find the actual person to catch hold of in
that way, hand holding the other's far heel
while

opening a space for them to move in.
Emerging from the path at the base of the
small bluff beside the lake, the
northeastern cove where the black-beaked
swans had gathered and were trumpeting
warbling tones, I stood face to face with
the largest of the three oaks. Two weeks
ago it had brown leaves. Now bare, I saw
where the trunk divided into three

massive limbs that formed the crown. A
fourth, nearly as thick as the others, looped
at the juncture sharply back into the tree's
body, and as I prepared to write that sight

of the fourth limb as wide around as a
person growing down into the fork, air and
water were visible in the lines and curves
flowing below the bark, green grass, air
bubbles below the ice, animal tracks beside
the things on the moon, the moon an
unnamed tributary that joined the river
where willows migrated across and the
bridge without a train stood overhead. I
crossed on the tracks. Don't fall don't fall

torn bark mouth fractured trunk mouth
mushroom mouth the air bubbles below
the ice near the holes in the ice the future
growing into the past and the past reaching
into the future language

begun in fields writing with gratitude
words that had migrated through so many
bodies in the snow on the ice seeing also
then in the cleared space of the letters the
air flowing below the surface

in shapes that also shifted. Things that
can't see being seen demanded speech and

touch. All this is in the text. At the body
of a dead merganser in the sand, the white
underbelly facing upward, I bent down and
pulled gently on a wing feather, refusing
the words that had come into me as I
reached toward it, that bird feathers carry
disease. Instead of coming loose, as I'd
thought or feared, the wing lifted and
spread. The light shone through the
feathers, changing them

from ashy gray to silvery lead. I shuddered
when the head turned toward the wing as
I pulled on it and forced myself to note the
gravel that had collected in the socket. The
eye was the only part I saw to be missing.
What were we doing at this moment last
week? Akhmatova said fade instead of
reach but reaching does burst in and one
does live all over again

surrounded by reeds trampled into a path
between the narrow wood and the frozen
creek, here by people, there by animals, by
the wind, and one can walk through them

into a clearing where grass clippings are dumped and leaves also. The cardboard square of a pizza box changes the light so dramatically, the clearing is an interior, artificially lit.

TiP
TOE
SOT

Found two pebbles in the small bays that form
between the ice floes.

Stood ice sheets in the snow to spell THE BOOK
and then by the river mouth used pebbles from
the bay to write OF PEBBLES in the snow.

While I knelt in the snow with handfuls of
pebbles and set them one by one to make the
stems of the letters or dribbled the smaller
pebbles into stems 2 or 3 pebbles wide, I heard a
sheet of ice from the jam break free and then saw
it float out the river mouth into the lake. Caz said
she and her sister acted out stories from books
and movies as children and experimented with
how small a change was sufficient to change the
story. A mountain undulates

and I experience peace even as ontologically
ripped. The snow disappears in the sun under
water, the mountain then moves. I hear the
strange moaning sound I heard in the night, and
then I hear it subside. The bird tracks, very faint,
a small bird, a scrawl bird and the seagull tracks
that began, made a right turn and ended.
Monday the deer tracks

separating in lines descended the hill. Squirrel
eating a strip of mulberry bark twists it as if
writing or tying a knot. Sand in the driveway
to melt the ice, potting soil on the neighbor's
sidewalk, black with white beads. The river was
running fast in small waves with snowmelt and
flicked back by the roaring south wind. Between
the houses the lake is smaller than the roof.
Alyson sang "Come Away, Death" at rehearsal
and the room

the silence of the room around a singing voice a
still singer gave me a chill in response to the
space suddenly tangible, propriocepted, part of
the body. Afterwards in her office she read me a
funny letter from Lamb to Wordsworth, how
Lamb didn't care if he ever saw a mountain
and then a letter from Lamb to a friend, "four
sweating pages" from Wordsworth. The poems
are good he says, but he doesn't want to be
forced to eat. Tears in eyes talking about school,
"Mont Blanc," *Villette*, class, but I don't know
what kind of tears they were,

the happiness and sadness of a small thing inside
a large thing and the small thing larger still. The

bottles in the mini-fridge rattle as the compressor
ins-and-outs, I was radiant walking without a
limp noticing the flecks of yellow warning paint
ground by feet off the stairs mixed with a
scattering of lavender salt meant for the ice that
was no longer there on the landing. A phrase
repeats then the room rotates slowly around the
eyes. An itch in the palm is a narrow pin going in
and out while the sunlight through the hackberry
and the eyelid

coruscates inside the eye. Making present
something not present can be perverse,
perversity a type of lie, and so it is in kind
with overacting while acting is the thing itself
including pretending, pretending itself.
Hölderlin says tragedy is fire and the
commingling of size and no size, though he says
god + human or human + nature, and a rage at the
oneness, which leads to separation. It's all one I am
thinking. When the man in #7 stopped talking

I noticed a completely different relation in the
sound of the train whistle than I had to his voice.
Beep of a car being locked, cars passing,
unidentified hum, crackle in right ear, seagull

shriek. Without names a locus of sensations.
A fir tree behind a house grew out of the roof.
The house a horse with a green-cloaked rider.
Northern shovelers a pair in the sun at the
widening open water

out the mouth of the river, the male brown white
green blue, female mottled brown, the bills very
wide and tilted down, swam out past a branch
meeting its reflection at three points going into
the water. A bird flies out of the hemlock tree
interlaced with the mulberry tree and I see the
sun in the river blown upstream and a

canoe floating down through my armpit. Two
woodpeckers land in the maple, circle the
circumference of a branch and ascend. This is a
scratchy somatic picture of the pain + tightness
in my body right now + earlier, left glute meeting
hamstring, band across lower back, right calf,
left shoulder. When the body doesn't align itself
to the page and the page doesn't align itself to the
body, when the alignment isn't

complete, there is a conversation. A finch
balanced on the gutter, then the O of wood

dangling from a wire, then the clothesline, then
the basket of sticks, then the wind chime, and of
those things the moveable ones, clothesline, O of
wood, wind chime, basket of sticks, began

this way and that in the energy transferred from
the body of the finch. Celery, the knife thumping
the board, the shadow of the hemlock moving on
the still curtain, I am thinking of the December
day the snow piled on the head of a cardinal a
thistle a tulip a goldfinch. A man in a gray hood,
a woman in a black hat, a leaf

running up the sidewalk behind them. Yesterday
by the river Lisa said she needs to make a will
and when I woke James to dress-rehearse *Lear* he
said he in a dream was measuring his script with
a ruler and counting his

cats. I think I was making a will, he said.

After he ate we sat on the daybed opposite ends
facing one another to do lines, the first third of
Lear. He put his feet on my stomach because they
were cold. He told me he's noticed how
susceptible to flattery Lear is throughout the

play, the slightest kind word from the Gentleman
and he changes his mood. Where is it dark
enough to see the Milky Way? Something loves
hearing how

snow leaves itself comes back settles then
departs. O the books—trees complement growth
of many things and also tip to toe and then a
book on Tao how great spirits in the region of
lakes + rivers become lake + river spirits. The
gods come down + then aren't gods but the things
that come down in the nerve endings deciding
not to move.

Sot, of all things, each has crystals and will be
seen according

to that array. A man who can't sing well will sing
freely, not knowing where he errs; a man who
sings well is bound to do so. Suppose the singing
birds musicians, several of the Ss backwards in
the field, the willow tree is longer than

the first-Wednesday noon sirens begin, one a
second after the other, so rising and falling pitch

is dissonant, at its loudest moment, with its
selves divided.

Lear covered in ferns last night in place of rank
fumiter and furrow-weeds and today his hand
holding two small sheets of ice held stuck
together, the point of the ice about to touch the
water where the reflected hand had its natural
hues, earth tones oranges

pinks browns, and the one in the air burned or
rather dazzled in the eye, erasing itself in me
who looked. The moment he leaned forward
from the Fool's question, Thou canst tell why
one's nose stands i' th' middle on 's face?

another world appeared, something he'd find in
the grass, an ant or a mouse, he'll bend to it later,
between the actors and the audience, the stage
and the seats, and it is in that place

he sees he's done wrong, sees his mistake as an
overlooking of that space, the same one Cordelia
feels when she refuses to speak, into which she
speaks her refusal, which found its voice in the
howl,

Howl, howl, howl! directed at the stage as Lear
carries her back through that space and feeling the
life in it makes that sound. But it is also there
facing the audience, leaning out and over her,

the feather moving where the glass doesn't fog.
The mouse it is

Lear bends down to see better and then to feed.
The wood duck opens and closes his beak rapidly
between the muskrats and the mallards. The
female has white around her eyes that come to a
point and she is the first to climb out onto the ice.
The power line and the mulberry branch are
vibrating but I can't see a creature. Book, opening
its words, knew hidden particulars of how

contained happiness dreaded fastening a year
where it lay, year summer became compressed,
little year of indolence tightly wound. Variable
melodies I heard as vulnerabilities last night when
Skye said it. The shadow of my spiky hair is large
on the wall and when I raise my eyebrow the
eyelash flickers. The angle of the light tilts the
large shadow of the bed knob toward me. Caz

said after vibrational moments, a fairy that might
have been a bird darting behind a tree, she turned
to the dry

leaves piled on the ground or I turn to the room
wrapping around itself in the convex reflection
on the doorknob, a switch in polarity, the
ordinariness of the fairy darting behind the tree,
the vibrational moment of the leaves. Insects on
log, insects waking the bulb, a trial lily, ants
walking and talking there beside a tree, letters,
ants, then letters, and then

the ringing in the ear is certainly inside the ear,
the swallow in the throat is inside the throat and

is noise ordering each anticlimax upon thee,
telling thee the watching fed my tongue glass,
lips, young, last year's primrose stalk bending in
the breeze, the hemlock-broken light on the mat
where I lay on my back on the floor, a blue tarp
flapping on an old school worktable, another
rescued from the dumpster, the

tarp held down by a crate, to write this list, the
shadowed troughs and crests of a wave moving

under the melting ice that otherwise appeared
flat, goldeneye, two buffleheads, northern
shoveler, nettles and animalcules in the rood the
yarn promised me. The flesh holds hands below

leering, and coincident keeps drifting. My
absolved caterpillar, your legion legs are
presupposed, the poetics of continuity will
deliver the mayfly, good insect, peaceful insect,
opportune at grief's bitter upswelling. The
butterfly began one week, folded before it
compassed, is that contumely? Howling grief,
the welkin's shoulders move. Ground felt

an eager toe. What do with agony? Move, hardly
move, mention the agony, count peas in a pod,
and italicize all answers? The shower hum in #7
comes on. The black ink on the left index

finger is again before the page and alongside the
page. A half-moon, yellow gray, on the north

wall from the large porthole on the south, street
light and opening

an opening in the opening of the throat allowed
descent into the body. A big thing, the sensation
of entering one's body, already one's and yet it

swells on entering and in the swelling rises and
also enters collapsing and weeping. I am thinking
(and as it happens it happened) of those deep
intakes of breath that follow long periods (hour,
minute, day) of not breathing, as if breathing
hadn't happened, and the fear that follows that I
might never breathe again or so rarely breathe or
that so much of my life has passed in long barren
intervals with hardly a breath. The sun warming
the air

makes the light on the blanket waver, a smoke
shadow, and when I look closely at these rising
shadows of air molecules the blanket trembles
without moving and I tremble beneath it without
moving.

Wild animals move and move, move slowly, how
they will go with

nothing, even lighter, with the event shrugged,
hearing you juggle reasons until you shut the hole
in the event. Teeth finch robin fish

the body in a wetland the size of the body a river
flowing in at the mouth, a rabbinical commentary
question design red-winged blackbird trill a
rolled *R* collecting ROCKS in Cape Breton by
walking to the sea. Nine allows an integration,
ten returns ten, yolk plus man then flies fiddling
here here "It's been a long time" isn't there

in the index of first lines because it's part of
something larger so I am flipping through from
back to front to find it there it is the first line on
the page it is the first line of. The ice island
pushed by the east wind found a tone arm in a
willow tree branch hanging down a little in the
water lifted by the ice and thwump thwump
thwump the tone arm willow played

the ripples on the ice deepened by melting. A pair
of wood ducks with flock of mallards is that
mistaken? The rare duck has almost the same
colors as the common, the arrangement of the
feathers into a helm crown and a white line
tracing the edge of the opening for the face
makes the distinction.

There isn't any time coming out of the sun now.

One has answered yes to what may never emerge
is yet here noticed not missed. If now patterns
yell, entering all in all,

here come your ponies, li and la and yearning yet
said how the world goes.

Clothes on the line

reflected in the window waving in the wind
white clothes that then flapped to dark shirts and
pants against a white sky. A dozen robins below
the three large oaks on the hill yesterday. I
brought a twisted stick home from behind the
feed mill and made Lear

running off with no boots. I didn't know that till
a bird shadow and then another flew over his face
while I was

writing a letter. Lately have you played your part
then laid your concerns down then I, you, hazard
welcomed, feeling it increased your compassion,
hop or pirouette or stumble into it, noting yellow
sun or Italian yellow composed sea, naked once
the wind grew mountainous, took in hand her
movement of vowels. Whole year held ground,

made stage creature live on faith. An ephemeral
wall of ice bricks began to drip more melodiously
where it was balanced on the branch before it
collapsed. Four mergansers and several pairs of
geese gliding on the very still lake. River mouth
had opened, leaving a hairpin turn on the south
side and the water flowing out along the long
narrow spit on the north. Where the bank had
collapsed a large root in the sand above projected
out

two feet down toward the gravel below. Monday
I walked with Jordan in the rain and he showed

me two swans, tundra or trumpeters, the latter
rarer and larger. He thought trumpeters—a
yellow line by the eye, I think he said, U instead
of V in the curve of the beak,

but also said that's what he wanted to see. The
mergansers go south, turn for a nonce, move
behind the head. My being hesitated feeling it
must be here within the territory. Pouring out a
full beer in the parking lot beside the beach, a
police says, "But it was open, you just didn't
have time to drink any," while the driver is patted
down by the other. Then the police returned to
Spanish, then English, then Spanish, deciding
when to let the man he'd stopped understand
him. I listened, loading the bricks in the trunk,
considering which words to write

in tiny letters on paper to be placed behind the
bricks and read through the holes. The art of our
necessities is strange I thought. Alyson said the
magnificent frigate bird appeared near Fort
Myers unusually, a consequence of global
warming someone told her. Bojan said after
framing houses all day he'd sit by himself in the

bar while the others complained, he reading
Euripides rather than retelling

the shitty day he'd already lived once. The style
of speaking through the armpit to the sky. I said
sometimes the initials make a change in the flow
because of the introduced structure but other
times the seams weren't so visible. There was
a loon lying low in the still water of the lake I
knew was a loon when it dove under and didn't
return. 7 leaves and a stone

are resting in the bird bath. Tonight it's going to
rain. Stepping past the cottonwoods the sun near
setting hit the coots' beaks and the beaks glowed
white and the last ice visible below the bluff
glowed a mile behind them. The full moon
appeared later, the same color as the top half of

a cloud. When I learn how to walk, and stand,
and breathe, I will be a

child, I told somebody. I thought of saying
"again" and also of writing "again," but it

wouldn't be correct I thought. As I faced a large
tree trunk, almost orange in the late light, I saw

how the trunk twisted clockwise around its
center (the hollow path around which the whole
thing curved is in there somewhere I am
thinking) and then

then met a huge branch that twisted counter-
clockwise tight against the main trunk and I am
looking at an inside, I thought, an inside known
by the divergent twists of its outside. I was
feeling the way it twisted in my own body

twisting to look in a mirror at the back of my
head that led out to the honeysuckle, corn field,
lowest muddy corner where hadn't been before
and coming back down the gray cat by the
brown-eyed susans purred no more. Nothing
provokes

Lear, nothing transforms him, nothing allows
him to be with Cordelia at the end. We talked
last night about how the motives for the action of
the play are

discarded + forgotten as unreal. The child is for a
time my child. We share a physical existence in
the moon on top of the lake, two loons known
diving under, Lear responsible but free of cause
and effect at the table while we share a soft
pretzel and three mustards. The telescope
showed the white spot at the top

of the moon extended a little out from the
surface. We heard a loon with our ears in the
world where we were flesh and blood. The brick
beehive hut beside the pile of discarded bricks is
hollow inside, four feet wide, four feet tall, an
opening at the top the size of a face, and the

sun is visible in the interior through the gaps in
the courses. A beagle walks by, I hear a cardinal
whistle six times, now seven eight it is hard nine
to ten finish eleven a sentence. The

counted whistling was coming from a very
white-breasted red-headed woodpecker

climbing, striking, and whistling toward me on
the hackberry branch while the pen runs out of

ink and the notes sometimes strike in time with
the head. Where does he go? Bits of white
honeysuckle catch the light, the bird lands on

the upsidedown cedar trunk painted black red
and green in spots six years ago. Dear yard
containing nuts, maples, negative space, nettles,
walls, masks, the sculptures there, loitering time
made thee, something says help or promises that
intrinsic motion announces

salvation, the hand, foot, skin I touch. First the
drunken boat is free of trade and then later free
of prison hulks—between, the drunken boat
sinks into the sea by looking down into the stars
reflected, finding a bay of phosphorescence. To
write the eye in beloved one must subscreyebe

to the iam. A trio of ducks surfaces though I
didn't see them duck under on my way to get
linen thread to bind notebooks with Jordan. The
bean vine is a black eye on a red field, an I, eye.
When counting the sounds, tumtitums, sa sa sa,
tra la la, give sounds the option to

multiply linked sounds, the noun heard ankling
my boot, sounds wed grasshopper stitch to
drakes necking there including a mistress to hear
less means hearing is held down. I saw Mr. Yu
pass in front of the car and studied his walk to
see how I might safely move. A mallard head in
the sun was

blue then green when I changed the line. I
thought, I'll wait for the donkey, an apple stick,
to say his name. The paper grain. A sardine is a
poem a bean a

pebble a real thing a last time a kinglet the inlet

of the river now is moving south in a long narrow
channel of sand before it empties into the lake
completely and completely continues. There
was a portal on both sides of the fold Madi made
and she knew but the kids in the canoe didn't.
Five pebbles beside the bed three two five one.
Yesterday with Jordan walking on the beach
I found two large bones, scapulas perhaps,
a moose's horn

before I realized it was a bone, an interior that
also had an interior, a webbed dark structure
full of space in pockets. The storm a storm had
brought it out of the pebble bank. The bone was
green and in the smooth cup of the joint the
green was webbed with dark black lines. The
second bone was the first bone I thought, two
left hands from the same man. Four small
avocados two bananas a can

of low-sodium lentil soup two chocolate bars
English

muffins. Daisy are you still working at the
grocery store? Lisa when will I see your sardine
poem? James do the other eyes have beans? The
pain comes and goes, dry land, wet land
intermediate across the

fold where I dreamed I had a key in my back
pocket for tightening furniture in the press bed.
A mundane dream is a real thing, full of the
energy of confusion. I sang come away death. A
tongue and then a spit of land I walked to the end
and turned around. A brick that is a little off-

kilter slowly reveals the energy of its structure.
Ground found bound in lines as poems. The
words I wrote a minute ago are upsidedown on
the left-hand page, the notebook turned for
writing back to the beginning. At the base of a
large willow by the bridge I noticed two dozen
suckers cut back to an inch, green bark

flecked with gold. Who are you? I said to the
birds in the reeds behind the construction-site
berm and they very quickly [hermit thrushes]
flew away. She said my spinal mobility has
increased from 1 to 2

plus. Three is normal. "June 29. Brecht speaks
of the epic theater; he mentions the children's
theater in which errors of presentation,
functioning as alienation effects, give the
performance epic features. With small
companies something similar can happen. I recall
the Geneva performance of *Le Cid*, at which the
sight of the king's crooked crown gave me the
first idea of the book on tragedy I wrote nine
years later," Walter Benjamin

writes in his Svendborg notes of conversations
with Brecht. Lying on the ground meditating I
saw a man turn left but the right side of his body
continued on and a column of smoke came out of
his shoulder. He became a woman in a dress bare
at the shoulder with a glowing red knot of ribbon
above each ear. They had been the man's eyes.
This seemed to repeat a dream I'd had when I
went back to bed at 5:30 having gotten up at 2:30.
The sensation of half my

body getting up and the other half refusing to

release it so it snapped back into place. Twice the
pen came through from pauses on the recto,
written last Sunday when the notebook was
moving toward the end as now back toward the
beginning. A steady snow, at a slight angle east to
west, and the flakes that come a little back cross-
hatch + make it double, a crooked crown.
Swirling gusts add snow from the roof + the
arbor-

vitae across the street has its branches lifted and
then slapped against themselves as the tensility

draws them back. Among the conversations,
Benjamin records his own dream, of a labyrinth
of staircases, from which many people fell. One
willow makes many strands under weaving.
Naming

demands brevity, a newt tongue. What's before,
what after? Each daisy, some asters, so flowers
the pasture. "Once, what made me start up was
no dream but a night train, which sped by with
an enormous din, scarcely a step from the
parapet." Handke, *Repetition* That sentence

gave its first letters. If it is betrayed, what was
betrayed turns out to not be the thing itself,
which continues in a new form that can be
touched and met unaccompanied. A hill of tiny
purple and later tiny yellow flowers last Sunday
now under the snow I am thinking. Yesterday
someone shouted when a goldfinch landed

in the lilac outside the dining room window. I
wasn't quick enough to see it but I did see a flash
of yellow in the room. When I reached the
window I noted the gold-green buds of the lilac.

A moment later the bird or another goldfinch
landed on the bare grape vine and in the gray
atmosphere and the snow just beginning to fall
the yellow and black of the bird grew larger and
more detailed, down to the filaments of the
feathers.

A weird drone making my arms tingle chimes
within its cone.

It wasn't the antipoem reading that made me
laugh and spit on the table not only that also
a sudden lightness rising from the stomach
through a force field in the chest and out the ears
nose and mouth, the same excess the osprey
didn't see, the seagull didn't, the northern
shoveler when I ran with the camera in my
hand from fifty feet to thirty feet did see it the
northern flicker didn't see it while I crept until
it did then fled down the very path I followed
fleeing before

me or moving or opening the way before me but
then when I said hello

to the kinglet that didn't flee I also laughed it isn't
fleeing or the lack thereof but something else the
sensation I have crept then dashed or crept and
crept and entered the body I am before I take
another step. The falling freezing rain in straight
lines is visible against the dark green of the pines.
The cattail fluff didn't absorb + bond

with the casting slip but shed it as feathers will.
One attached single word object verb hammock
snow ash flow of the water over the rocks after
the thin layer of topsoil washed off leaving beds
of seed stones that later fell out of my pocket.
These initials will propose loss while murmuring
middle tones until tomorrow arrives. Arrival
sweet cowbell flowers lay heads somewhere high
dingdong and juniper

trees blooming and falling. Inside the cave of
sheared rocks looked down through a square of
light to the pasture where we stood and looked
up. Why the heavy sad feeling sweeping the sand
off the steps at home and then lying

near the river in the sun? Each last breath is full
of life, I thought. The scrawny cat in the yard
this morning made me think of

Purr the cat was gray who died around this day
15 years ago. A box of onion skins in the barn
there

was where I found the book called *Trees I Have
Seen* Lisa put into her book, the cave inside the
cave I just read inside a tale inside a book. That
could be wrong but I remember it. A minute
before, "That the soul of our grandam might
haply inhabit a bird" had passed through not
seeing the starlings, but writing them down and
in the final clause as I felt the sentence

not ending, I thought, the care I felt inside the
parody of catechism, in the play of changing
identities, that care fails when attached to a
particular name or embodiment. A serious
observation of one thing after another is a loving
action. The last dry blossom petal on the
hydrangea outside the round porthole south-

facing motel window vibrates in the northeast
wind that swings the branches of the pine
southwest and then by the force of the flexing
wood the branches return past the point of rest
and swing again. Daisy saw Megan digging a
piece of bark out of the green ash, the fallen ash
that fell southwest down the slope from the grass
into

the strip of woods that leads down to the
riverbank. It was the ash Megan pulled the sign
off and Daisy saw in seeing those actions a
possible way into the tree's interior and wanted
to follow. Then Madi, who'd been leading us,
came back out of the huge

cottonwood trunk into the light of the bridge.
My chest tightened when I saw a car beside #7
and a light in the window, and then heard raised
voices. "She isn't even here," a woman was
saying, but then it isn't a problem to have people
on the other side of the wall from where I am
sleeping. A transitory person I took on made the

world one for a while, playing both hearts with a
heartbeat and kinship of place, time, mundanity

in the continuous onrushing imagined joy. Then
when nouns appeared,

pinecones in heaving foot to toe, water moon
divided, overarching of an excited sound, duck,
woods, opening of the ash, the wooden ankle
accessed on slipping off anguish, Megan's hand
below forest, tree, root, ovary, follicle, triune,
the white-band-on-the-neck black ducks diving
below the breaking waves and the flock of
long-billed

waders where the river empties out that flew
away at my approach but then returned and
stayed and the two in the river behind the woods
where the ash tree fell, thin-necked and head
black-brown, a little gold crest on one, I don't
have any other names for them. When I first lay
down a gentle pulse of the space inside or just
below the skin replaced thought, was both
attention and its object. Megan and I talked
about

fiction, construction of a narrative feeling from
fragments, the seriousness of the fragments, a
coherence practice that is the laying bare of the

device of coherence practices, liberating them
from operating in the dark, below the surface, or
allowing them to operate in the pulsing fall,
wholly

below the surface instead of a small corner
subroutine of the several networks. Though
there's not a heating pad behind me I feel, as
often in recent weeks, heat radiating into my
lower back from whatever it is pressing against.
Megan objected to the statement a visitor made.
Presence is dynamic and various, I think she was
thinking, not the guaranteed outcome of a single
practice. The chime isn't playing but I hear it in
the fan of the heat exchanger. Antiwriting was a
manifested delirium. It

exchanged the task. Hours hold days in between
trees, the evening said. Riding to PT it occurred
to me, as I looked at the half-finished buildings
on East Wash., that F. has the same relationship
to poetry. Of poetry she said to me recently, this
takes discipline, to be so focused, and then I
thought one thing at a time has importance for F.

and these shifts in focus are so complete as to
make impossible, for their duration, the thought
or belief or memory of a time when this wasn't
the place of composure. I took comfort in this; it
is the quality she showed me first, of seeing what
is there, seeing an aspect of what is there I should
say, more

completely than anyone, I thought, and the
impermanence of the attention (an
impermanence she shares with everyone,
however we disguise it) is not a measure of its
weakness, but a feature of its strength, and a
potency of return. All years made sensations of
sun and wind and however hours betrayed a
sensation and took all in, real time continued
opening filiations where now you can go naked,
the words sewn on every body by hand. The
light from the northwest window for

the first time this spring is casting the fluctuating
shadow of a thickly branched shrub come into
leaf onto the wall above the sheep stone and the
orange crystals

balanced on the slice of oak rescued from the wood piled by the path-clearing men imprisoned by the state. The shadow is so far from its source the branches and twist are indistinct and overlapping, a translucent forest, the shadow a source of heaviness and light. A robin in the hemlock drops into flight and I see the white tail feathers as they spread. Bitter interior time,

I too hear patterns and tremble. Once James and I showed a geologist a fossil of fish scales, a bit of a fin he said, adding that a fossil is just something that has been replaced with something else, grain by grain, perhaps in a stream bed a million

or eighty years ago. I hear a robin. The little black beetle on my pant leg rolls into a dot when I try to wipe it off. There's blood from cuts after carrying the hive-shaped crystal home from the beach, years later revealed to be a froth of volcanic glass suddenly hardened, a body of vesicles, the geologist told me, as in a cloud or soap bubbles

I am thinking I can't write this all down.

That the feeling that speaking and listening are
the same thing + other bodies—

That writing is a kind of sixth or seventh sense

in the motion of my hand when I am writing
quickly and it exceeds my imagination of it, the
out-of-body experience of watching the hand be
me my body. I also feel my head swell + lighten,
vesicular, the plus lighter even than the
ampersand and a very pleasant neutral sensation
in the body, the neutrality of not having parts but
just being a body, a hand. Words were things
before they became ideas and grain

by grain become things again. I thought about the
periodic table of the elements when I came in. I
said hello. Hello linnet, be named.

When big and little drop away in relation to
things

some pain a mayfly on your arm

the writing hand below the text falls and is lifted
over and over by the letters and the hand in

moving stays blank and is moving to be to make
to

be out from under the letters, the lake flies
coupling on the table beside the crystal-cloud-
hive. No size, no size. The tale outside the body

leaves a blank buzzing, the stairs I walked down
every Beach Aire day last year lost its lower half
into the clay-and-gravel collapsed face of the
bluff on its north side. I hear a truck, robin, a
cardinal, a truck, a red-winged blackbird
warning call, the pen and the page, the breath in
the nose, then throat, then lungs, then back
cracking. Megan wrote then said the thinking of
writing is a blank buzzing of thoughts available
only at the moment of,

in the whole of the thought, and I am thinking a
single word, the only one there in what remains a
series, a buzzing blank on either side as it is
written. The actor knows the one word they are
saying or the syllable or listening. The many
small cuts fine white lines on the surface of the
hands from the many fine slivers are gone this

morning. A shimmering blue-black backed
shimmering insect falls on my shirt and rolls up
into a point. A mosquito

bites my knuckle. The bloodroot had opened
yesterday but now completely, a red-inside-green
stem below eight white petals in a spiral with
space between them attached to the yellow
center. A black-and-white warbler ten feet away
on the bluff tree where the kinglet had been and
is. Today I learned

its name and form. What did the name do to the
bird I was thinking seeing it apart from black and
white on the in and out of tree bark that also
crosses back and forth.

Necessity

Trying to hold the pen so gently to the paper that only the ink made contact, I am attempting to continue a story I have yet to begin. I don't think, "an owl counts its vocalizations" but "a duration coming into being and passing away and coming into being again." When do you feel most alive?

Lately the feeling of the brush end of the pen has seemed too inexact, as if something is being lost, though when I look up at the *L* in *Lately* instead of loss I see the fine lines of the individual fibers of the brush separating from the others just enough to show 8 or 9 years later it seems to have been made

by other people and we are seeing them with our two ears, hearing them with our two eyes, saying them with our open nostrils, smelling them with our two hands, writing them with our two mouths. Last night after I sent Max those five

film stills I kept watching *Rome, Open City* and soon after the woman, Pina, in the scene with "Max," I shot and killed running after him as the soldiers take him away and her son, who has just accepted "Max" as his new father—they were to be married that day—is crying and

screaming in the street. I felt ashamed I'd sent it, as
if I'd again acted before thinking, before knowing
what I was doing. The subsequent scenes filled me
with terror, a terror at grief, and have been
returning and shaking me this morning. I see I wrote
"I," "I shot and killed" where I'd meant to write "is,"
"is shot and killed." The boy, 7 or 8, is inconsolable,
wild, flying into the air

with grief as a person tries to hold him back. A
non-professional actor, the boy, I wonder how he
experienced that terror and that release. Last night
I was afraid you'd get it and know what happened
next and be upset that I wasn't thoughtful and then
this morning I feel a kind of duty

to let you know. It's a strange situation, neo-realism,
with its documentary scenes of life in the streets and
amateur actors, what I've been trying to write. Your
letter to Italy asked, What can be told without
harm? This morning

you answered, "There's no harm done (in my
opinion!) to the actors, director, editor, or even the
characters who are trapped in that one tragic

narrative, no harm done if you free those characters for a minute, let them live another life than that single one, let their path lead elsewhere—to my place! To where you and I meet. Let them be with us there." Adding, rearranging, and reducing all relieve one of the illusion

one knows what one means, what one has written, how one's life came to its present, one's world, and a result with sufficient integrity and independence might prevent one from clinging to it still. My father said he's afraid "that's it. This is what it's going to be like from now on," or after a good day, "this can't last." A *kri-king* sound

I heard today in a clear Chiwaukee Prairie pool. My first peeper of the spring I said out loud. "Each time I brush this singular horizontal line [*ichi*] I cannot avoid thinking how absurd it is

to keep repeating this same foolish action over and over again. But then I realized that I may be incapable of doing anything but foolish actions, and again today I drew the number one." The right ear rings,

numb nose, space above the eye socket expanding.
A budded sucker at the base of a cottonwood, red
sheathed in white. I sneezed after "might" and
waited a moment for the words to slow down and
return to where the pen was waiting to write them.
The newspaper pages flopping over in the drainage
swale seemed to switch instantly from great weight
to airy lightness

as the strong wind held them vibrating in the grass
then lifted them into a tumbling flight. We're in a
small apartment with Norman Mailer. He's telling F.
how wonderful she was for him. "You were my
youth! My youth came back to me through you!"
He's hugging her and exulting. "I've met many
people in my life," he says to me, "but she is a rare
spirit." I tell him I know, but that his time is over and
he should leave, that he's beginning to be seen

as an old buffoon. He accepts this, but as he leaves
he points to the harlequin mask on the bed. "I'll
leave now, but don't forget what part you'll be
playing." He mimes holding up the mask and says,
"My lady." "Our favorite play," I tell him, ushering
him out the door, feeling the great tenderness

between Olivia and Feste. Paint flecks on the wood
floor

mark where a wall divided this room in two. The hip
flexors and psoas stretch and release in the steady
rhythm. Balanced in a shadow at a stop light, the
fine dry snow blown from the warehouse made
vortices in the sunlight and then a bus going by,
dozens of people sitting peacefully in the other
world

and not alone! "'Galeotto fù il libro, e chi lo scrisse.'
'Galeotto was the book, and he who wrote it.'"
Separating the legs at the knees, defining and feeling
the separation even when the calves and feet folded
underneath press against the thighs and buttocks,
gluing the cracked neck so the neck can be extended
and the excess of the face sawed off. One and then
after a long delay another

milkweed seed flew off into the breeze. For five
years daily meditation practice + notebook writing,
observation practices, the nonhuman world, the
human world, the domestic human world, the
overlapping world, the theatrical world, the textual

world, the dream world—Peace, peace. The waves
ran over the high edge of the beach,

flooding the plain and soaking my shoes as I failed
to run between them. "Even a drop of ink from
the brush can form an ink-play. As you move the
brush freely across the scroll, there is no true
depiction. Yet you are suddenly aware of a finished
work—spring in its abundance." Wide awake at
two a.m., I read Proust and a sentence compared
something to an actress who arrives

early at the theater and pauses for a moment among
the empty seats in her ordinary clothes to watch her
fellow actors rehearsing on the stage. Is it that one
can survive so much loss? That the writing can? The
cries of hundreds of starlings not in that tree or that
tree or that tree but each branch

widened and darkened at the tips and more starlings
landed and the sound grew. The light shapes in the
blue curtain move to their tune. What part of your
life expresses necessity? I opened the window and
put my head out into the pine to listen, then into the

yard at two a.m. and heard nothing and faced away
from the sea and into the hill whence the owl
emerged following a road around a curve

so acute that to ascend one returned the way one
came. "Once while listening to my stereo, on
impulse I stopped the music and turned the amp up
to full volume. The air in the room changed as if its
presence had been multiplied. Space is not simply
the sense of distance to an object or how large
something is; rather space is a high-tension, zero-
sum, 'no-escape' situation in which any action
instantaneously results in the creation or
destruction of something." When I looked up the
sentence later it read: "Sometimes in the afternoon
sky the moon would pass

white as a cloud, furtive, lusterless, like an actress
who does not have to perform yet and who, from the
audience, in street clothes, watches the other actors
for a moment, making herself inconspicuous, not
wanting anyone to pay attention to her." Walking
through the grass, I picked up a cup thrown from a
car. In the silence that followed, the large waves

broke far out from the shore and the white crests
flashed in the low sun. For days afterward I had the
feeling of stepping in then out

then in again. Listening to Norman Fischer I
recalled the attraction I had 20 years ago to his
project of writing that filled each day for a year the
page of a daily planner his father may have given
him and my inability to express

the attraction to him or anyone. Instead I asked a
question with a mix of emotions I am now unsure of.
Did his translation of the psalm that included in the
original, as he explained, the skulls of the enemy's
infants being dashed against the rocks, skulls
translated by him as flowers,

deny the violence of the original? I was angry at my
attraction being hidden, but I didn't know that—
this was years before I took up a daily practice, in a
different form, of which this is a part—but I was
also confused by his choice. I'd like to ask the
question again, without animus. Why, by what
process, had the infants

whose skulls were shattered against the rocks,
become flowers? F. said I am preventing atrophy,
a natural process. The hawk I'd seen land in a tree
flew out into the sun and the body glowed more
orange than red. I wrote M U in the snow, not
closing the O, so it stayed a U while I waited for the
moon that didn't appear. Sometimes shortening a
text is a contraction, sometimes a release.

This present tense

Counting the periods all through the opus, telling how the soles of my feet, light and rapid in the grass, a twinge in my shoulder and the edge scraping against my index finger

required space, but also an object to receive them, an object to make a body, a body to animate them, Bashō writes somewhere about a bead of dew sufficient to bend the lily. I thought of a horse checked,

forced to stay in terror as a train passed. The horse turns in a whirlwind under the spurs and Ursula protests, an anguished protest, naked and like a gull's shriek. To Gudrun's horror, a tightness in the chest or low throat extending into the gut, Ursula is outside herself, unable to concentrate, alone but responsible. The osprey again flew over clutching a fish. Beets are cooking,

potatoes, onions. I wanted to know how people moved their heads, what they wore, how exactly they spoke. Words can be repeated but people and actions hardly at all. One at a time

yellow-green leaves are falling off the maple. Two attached to a twig flop over like a paddle wheel, the light switching sides. I could hardly breathe or follow a breath in the time I sat. I want to acknowledge that. The water is flowing out of the rain barrel into the heap of last year's primrose stalks. Instead of cutting out the letters of TiP TOE SOT, a face on the sculpture appeared as the nose became smaller.

No more today.

Not the intake of air not that air that comes in but the whole change in the system that results. "They are both stubborn," Mom said,

when she couldn't go with Andy to the doctor, "stubborn or afraid." "Both," I said. Read *Bovary* then cleaned the kitchen + house. On the way to the fair with his eyes closed, "I must be about to crash

into something," he said while he walked with a slight quiver down the center of the sidewalk. The lake alternated flats and ripples, the right big toenail rubbed the callus where the small toe joins the foot, the pen ran out of ink. To be alive I see the weeds coming through the cracks in Mary's driveway bright yellow, wet green milkweed pods soft when stroked, two broken clothespins, the lost laundry brush, an underwear rag. The imagined feelings of others take a place in one's body, but can the erotic lead the fiction to where the two are

split into one? a slip of the tongue, which she affirmed, "Yes, exactly." Moving toward the correct process without knowing the steps beyond the moment of their doing, one feels one

two three four five six seven eight nine

dozens of samaras on the porch floor at once. "The flatness of no mountains is the blessing of realizing you are nothing," Max writes. The window washer across the street misses the ladder's bottom step. The best known samara is the maple key, also referred to as a wing nut. Saṃsāra is a letter away, a complete gliding through or flowing around. In the succession of days I'd lost

Go Out, *The Birthday Present*, *Acting*, and others. Stopping to see what's there had seemed to forfeit the present. But from age 4 or 5, F. said, she'd made many small books, though she couldn't say, and who could say, why. I didn't write anything except once or twice but I felt

when I was alone the world changed into itself and became
the rocks and trees the ideas the brass cannon in the sand

the transformation of these things the body forms around.
We told him to stop studying he agreed. Outside it was
hotter than the closed-up house

the hot night wind coming off the lake the paddle boat
tagged *abandoned property* washed up in the flood

we said we should take it out we pushed it it didn't move we
don't know how they breathe and live these modes of being
that pursue us. Thomas said his other mentor told him when
you arrive there

you don't need to carry any of what happened in the past
with you. He was drawn to that experimental theater.
After rehearsal he saw them sitting in a circle, looking one
another in the eye, saying exactly what they thought had
happened. It was something

he'd never seen. Brad turned a tottering circle clutching the
dog, Trapper, to his chest on slippery slanted moss cliff
path 50 feet above the rocks and water he didn't worry or
fall he scrambled up to the proper path. Jordan turned
around and crossed again the gap that made him feel

death close. Later I heard mourning in the bird songs he
performed. At this hour the angled window light sun makes
a rainbow corona around my thumb. I move my thumb

it is the page that receives it I move my hand I write this and
feel the edge of the chair the foot on the table waiting on
Hawthorne a dove

trying to keep the green things together. The concrete
planter can't reach, the larch reaches a map in the bark, the
very vivid movements of a person adjusting their clothes a
loose dress swinging the same people walk

back up Hawthorne Avenue and keep going a bus glides
past the 14 I think I should get on I have an alldayticket I see
the bamboo moving and the cougar in it setting my pizza on
the stairs to write each cell alive

pulsing in extremities heart beating hard stomach full of air
I couldn't release a droning thought too much too much I
noticed the rising panic and said to myself you are panicking
oh look that thought is repeating and the thought would
change to noticing and slow the body and the pulsing
returns as I write this and saying that it passes it passed it
helped but on the clock I saw OK that's two minutes OK I'll

sleep but something was awake that wouldn't sleep a man is banging metal

installing HVAC on the roof across the street I tried to watch television but I saw the faces of the actors moving on top of the characters' faces the faces going through that together a generous strange series of contortions between actions and sequences that required

me to move closer to the order of perception which is the book's order, the fictional order of orders where the time of sequence rearranged is the present. Double spruce trunks touching at the base grow farther apart in the heights as I descended into

Zigzag Canyon, the bark scratch sound at eye level a wren at ground level a many-bee hum from the steep meadow behind the fir trees

no more than a red blood cell in the artery did I know sometimes where I was but I was

propelled at those times without fear. Yesterday Andy died while my mother held his hand and told him it was OK my father held his other hand he twisted in pain said I'm dying

and then he was calm and looked in my mother's eyes and
spoke after a short time stopped breathing my mother told
me yesterday as I drove down the coast alongside

Tillamook Bay then inland to the moon and thought of
Andy in his boat in Newburyport steering us through the
marshes into the open I hear two waterfalls the surging and
sinking back over my left shoulder I see Mount Hood in its
glaciers a climbing flying grasshopper almost touched my
face while I was meditating leaning on a pine up here the air

the wings moved I felt I wrote learning where it was hard
to arrive to climb the sandy scree I slipped and fell but what
was hard, it was hard to not keep going on towards the end
while imagining looking back to see if it had happened. By
stopping

a three-trunked pine appears, the tallest trunk the size of
me the whole tree on a boulder, a small stone rolls down the
hill then the chipmunk that dislodged it follows

dear Andy you have died and I address you

thank you for addressing me

in letters and reading mine in one you said you studied
Russian literature

and it was very hard to learn the language and people told
you not to and you probably shouldn't have and you've
forgotten it all but not what you told me about Tolstoy's
contrariness and Dostoevsky and the nihilists and the
shoemaker you told me that you don't regret it

this present tense that refuses no one

a raven caws and then the waterfall surges back pierced by
the drone of a small plane yesterday one landed on the spit
of land where Nicky and Brad were digging clams and I was
admiring the light on the purple-gold ridges of a shell as I
put it in the bag and the plane landed on the

small grass airfield on the peninsula that makes Nehalem
Bay passing from our angle directly through the stand of
firs the waterfalls divide in the moss and find many ways
down the hill. Thomas told me once about the moon

rising and each day crashing into the earth it was without
progression few loved it. I wrote, Larch, I

recognize you. A friend told me about someone who timed his orgasm to coincide with squeezing through a hole in a cliff in Oklahoma that brought him out behind the waterfall he then stood under I asked if it was a spiritual thing for him or just? But it was definitely a ritual for him they said

I can't recall his name what leads the teacher to the sun on an old overgrown demonstration plot one leaf several stems sexual transformation tree calling itself achoo the teacher

at times an open text, I said to Lisa, a generative text in the posture softened face muscles hands gestures the students read and go on reading years after the books on the table have been transported into the underworld. The osprey was flushed by the frisbee from the cottonwood

and soon after stooped, crashed into the water and came up empty. Thomas said the teacher of shorthand teaches the making of marks, but each mark takes

a timbre of its maker, so none is master, student, mark or teacher, and the world continues to be completed not only in shorthand. See the note to Max about the moon, Andy, the shape of a journey. The Lynden crabs are darker purple. Tonight there is a frost warning. A kind of intimacy

gave events the possibility of happening, to make them
happen

not having happened—this is happening—in writing and
reading, all things repeating

the letters in the water appearing where the duckweed had
been stirred, the tiny leaves attached and floating closing
the spaces of the marks the quick brown bird swiftly in the
understory a dragonfly landing on the duckweed then the
trunk of a mostly submerged willow. Yesterday I was
writing about the body and today I was walking

down the platform beside the train to Kingston perceiving
my body as who I was hoping to enter at which point it
might no longer be mine and I was thinking on the plane
there is no body in fiction there is fiction in love there is no
body in love the body in love is not fiction. The blue sky the
dark street taillights indigo clouds in a Cerulean sky the
dark interlacing lines of the metal supports of the track.
We lay down once to read the sun

was shining in the southwest window the river window and
she gave up reading and we drifted in and out of sleep and I
put my hand for a moment on her face and she said no I like
the light I said yes the light through our eyelids sparkling

after it comes through the trees and she said so that's what
blind people see? and we laughed and I said blind people
don't just have their eyes closed but after a pause

we don't know maybe it is what the blind see some of the
blind see dark and light and some have never seen and how
can we who see light know. Trees beside the tracks in the
dark in the street lights fly past. The sound of Nancy's voice
after 40 years I knew

instantly from when I was 6 or 10, before she left Arn, Arn's
voice too, and the shape of his mouth. We spread Andy's
ashes in the woods

after Carrie, Jess, Arn, and Carl spoke. We covered the
ashes with pine needles, leaves, Carrie added a mushroom
and I some moss and green leaves, hoped the moss would
survive. We didn't mark the place. After everyone left,

Carl (Dad) went out for dishwasher tablets and Mom
(Carrie) and I talked about Andy, was he gay, he was, how
he never told, why was he alone, that they explored
together as children and again in recent years, that he liked
to build with us, that reading *Lear* he told her he cried for
the first time just reading.

His journals, looked into, move between weather reports, reports on mood, philosophy, over and over the question of how to continue drawing, writing, and music and how frightening a pause is in the making.

He says after playing various selves at work, at home, with no one to behave in a proper way for, he has no self at all.

Mom and I saw a nuthatch by the bay circling down a hollow tree. In the mud bottom of the tidal stream, the water followed a course at lowest tide back and forth within the contours of the banks, a winding within the winding of the river through the eelgrass and mud. Arn (Andy's brother, who said as we spread the ashes he never knew him) is drawing from memory the burned-down

Newburyport house he built in the seventies, having no photographs to copy. I don't feel myself writing this after reading some of A.'s journals. He observes the movement of his hand writing and I feel I am his motion, that he is generating this movement that produces that acknowledgment. I was moved by the weather—"hot again

today"—and that he'd just set out on a journey after many delays. A bibliomancy, A. wrote, gave his thoughts exactly, that human sexuality is not biological but fixed by chance, not by chance but for various reasons, falls by chance almost or reasons of situations or arrangements encountered in youth.

I typed A for I and saw how close they looked. It was something (bibliomancy) we both did regularly without the other knowing, which I continue. Yesterday Mom and I also heard a goat bleating and then saw the goat standing on the steeply peaked roof of the small house in its enclosure. There were two goats, but only one was bleating. We agreed the yard should be bigger. There were

chickens under pine trees. I'm in the lower half of a double-decker car. The platforms are at eye level when the train enters a station. Four cranberry bogs and a drainage pond a table with three chairs behind a pole barn and another chair on its back in the grass. More bogs and ponds that don't seem connected to any roads, a house whose driveway crosses the track. "Leave space between the dead and *I thought.*" Pink small red-maple

leaves, a white milk carton balanced on thistles, aspens yellow green gold orange, things only people on the train see. Can you have a plot without characters? A plot made by perfecting the sentences, the plot of the effort and ultimate failure to perfect, to distinguish between the three—plot, character, and sentence—four if you count the world, five the woman at her desk, six the creatures in the sea. Whitman is the name of this town in the Taunton watershed where a puddle holds one maple leaf. In Abington diamonds drawn on the platform in chalk, a white building with paint scraped off the shingles

leaving flecks I want to stop and read before the train drives on through tall pines, a house with a long yard, a cemetery, a long cemetery with a small pond, an old brick mill with a rounded corner following the road, window after window with two courses of brick between them. South Weymouth platform, pine needles and linden leaves, also called basswood,

metal horns on either side of the lamp-post. After we spread the ashes, Jess said a dozen times, "We went over it and over it, there were supposed to be three or four kinds of bread, but there's only one, and I don't even know what kind it is." And then she stopped saying it. Braintree platform, a pair of shoes

walking past. James is writing about Andrew Johnson, a bad president he said, and we wondered why my uncle, Andrew

Murray Johnson, was named after him. My mother said it
had nothing to do with the president. Her mother wanted
another girl and was going to name her Ann, so Andy was
as close as she could get. We did one scene twice. The first
time Kate hadn't started the camera soon enough, and the
second time I

kissed Max on the lips after I blew out the candles. I didn't
know when I turned my face up and out of the shot, but
that's what happened. The second time I didn't make a wish
but acknowledged to myself that there was one in the room
not wishing for anything.

My words are small today, in red, quick but legible, a
music in the forced air in the vents of this empty cul-de-sac
house now that the people are gone. There's a white fence
between the grass and the woods on one side and just a line
of logs laid on their sides on the other. I realized in talking I
did choose Max, Lisa before that, and Lewis, and Jordan,
Daisy, a few others, I chose James, in the feeling

that I had already been chosen, but the other person may
have had that feeling too, of being chosen, of receiving.
I didn't know that before. What does it mean to choose? I
kept having the feeling that the answer to one question was
also the answer to another, that the questions moved.

Hundreds of paintings and drawings seen only by the
artist, now three weeks dead. What can we make of them?
Walking east on Bay Road. The five p.m. sun shines on a
cloud bank over the water and the steep hill of Standish
Shore, the white dunes on Plymouth Beach, and the white
boats and wave caps. I have the feeling of those old light
floating lighter-than-air guitars. A Guild and a Gibson.
A great blue heron by the low-tide stream

winding inside the marsh channel flies out to the mud flats
and its body is reflected there in the wet sand. The pen
reads the letters on the page and moves the hand. Carrying
boxes full of drawings and books I kept thinking of Carl the
age I am now helping to carry my books up the stairs in the
South End, saying it was the last time. A self in the
drawings is pictured as the puppet or mask

a strong physical being holds at arm's length and studies.
The sail dwindles then expands. A puppet was once called a
"motion." A witch nicely told the poet, O fool, why undo an
injury? Can these things, these sounds, be seen in a person

in the state of being unrecognized, a person and artist,
unrecognized as seen, unrecognition of being that?

I rubbed my forehead with my hand, holding the open pen away from the skin.

Andy in one journal wrote about a drawing of a boy with a dragon conceived in an instant looking at a Tang Dynasty vase, the composition appearing in an instant (the same instant?) very different from the vase, the drawing coming quickly. He wrote, "It may seem like the illustration for a children's book, but it was real and impertinent."

Another note: The tears in his eyes when criticized scared his piano teacher "so she allowed me my slovenly ways." Then: "Hours of ecstasy practicing the piano."

"I have little interest in writing, but not doing so seems to leave me too often subject to moods I can't explain. . . . I very clearly saw my clock reading 5:49; and another time I saw the wall collapsing, as clearly and distinctly as if it were really happening."

The moments of happiness.

High notes of an opera singer enter under the door.

The woman at the fish shop put a lemon in the bag with the salmon.

Three Japanese prints—my mother said she stared at two in childhood trying to understand what they meant. Max stumbled

running but didn't fall and then repeated the running without fear and felt, truly, that I was ready to catch him as he flew off the stairs. A part of the stone foundation exposed in the stable, the lines and branching flow of rocks

piled into an even space, moments of pure agreement, going down to swim with James and Lisa the first night in Pioppi, running with Max, walking with my mother

just now, continuing up the mountain with James, sitting in the forest alone. One she wondered about was *A Dream*. A note said,

"Certainly by Hokusai." The woman dreaming being dreamed leans on two bundles of brush that seem at first to be her legs extending out. Her legs are folded beneath, an opening in the dress shows the calf pressed against the thigh, and the bundle becomes a second figure, folded over on itself, on whom she leans, and into whom she extends. A dragon is printed in the space of the sky so

the outlines are barely seen. In the second print a woman
with an inkstone holds a brush poised, and my mother
wondered where her limbs were inside the kimono, whose
folds are marked by lines the brush might have made and
recalled a children's book about a tsunami in Japan and her
fear during the hurricane in Gloucester, remembering the
children she'd seen swept away in the book,

how these things come together here.

Passo

No self is in control of everything in the body.
Nothing happens again. Things again. Things

begin. The grass of the water meadow reaches
our heads and the cow tracks meander to
wallows. A line worn in the slope by feet

high above guides us, a sign proclaims *via ferrata*
chiuso, the iron path, the path of war is closed, my
translation

I acknowledge, transporting the valley past the
structures built a hundred years before by people
under

fire never intending one secret name to know all
memories. Even being peaceful gives burning
thoughts for the evening violence. A huge silent
bird-shadow momentarily contains us, followed
by a strange whistling hum

throwing us flat in the dread that loads every
passing moment with the burden of being a step
toward doom or happiness. The glider fifty feet
above it follows the need to finish

falling away, the breaks between these things he
whistles, the tune intermingled with his
breathing and the waterfall of astral hums in
complete

ignordinance in the ordinary forest face of pines
too steep to climb down

without the trunks and roots. The floor creaks, it
could be him, the fly on the window

touching the glass makes six white dots, leaves
with them, comes back, leaves them, comes back.
They read the text to end without stopping,
partly remembered, and probably

incorrectly, very aware of the strange pattern of
ups and downs needed to write them. If one
dropped out, another stepped in

and read their sentences, pausing to watch the
gnats walk up and down the rough grain of the
windowsill's pine boards. Those who had read
the entire text were suffused even after

the verb had lost its object. She studied a single
tree in the meadow, a deciduous tree in front of
the wall of pines rising on the far side of the
river, and he

who had had that perception and formulated it in
words less precise felt something he had thought
of as inside himself inside her

being replaced by a rising tree of mist made
visible from the new angle. James said he loved
running down, thinking of nothing while seeing
the next place he'd put his foot in the scree field.
When I want you to talk that way

that's why I ask you those kinds of questions, he
said at the bottom. A tiny sharp pain in the left
buttock the right calf a shallow constriction in
the ribs and then the ribs opening out for this
green ridge

I resolved to say nothing and less did. In the
house at four it was hard to believe these things
had happened after which I usually do love what

is happening and keeps happening over the long
muddy raspberry field and cow field where the
cows lick us with long purple tongues
aggressively

they won't hurt you, profiles in the cliffs of passo
di entralais, the peaceful entrance I keep
imagining it means, a romantic

even when the topic is comic and pervaded by a
tone of elegiac longing where we thought of
sleeping in the grass but kept going

down the green escarpment to the hut the dry
spring the stream on the map farther down the
sweet tumbling ochre stones sound below water
in the center of the dry white ones

the milky way thickening the morning the white
apple flesh yellowing in the pan the hidden
woodstove flames what we are afraid isn't visible

often is, what we worry is isn't, that cloud a
horse a crab now a face like mine looking at the
clouds,

so much as griefs that do not come and outcomes
that never arrive. Exhausted happy staggering
and almost falling giving way rising up

the natural chimney fluttering like a
hummingbird a peregrine falcon above the
pinecone on the huge anthill a bee landing on the
yellow strap of the backpack might return but
wasn't essential. Nothing was

startled on the muddy trail in the very tall grass
of the seeping passo oberenghe by a butterfly
where he fell and lay there laughing and laughed
again to see his image remaining

as the grass flattened into what he looked like
having fallen. A bee touched the river, we helped
it out, dried ourselves in the sun

alongside it. The sticks in the river spun in the
eddies. No one won. The inner ear is half
elsewhere and tries to bring

the body back to where the milky white
milkweed sap burned my arms. I cut some down

to free the pine, sidewalk, blue pearmain, larch.
The larch is as small here as on the top of the
moon. A tiny tear in the blanket, an eyebrow

hair, dots of ink with comet tails. The grass that
crept over the sidewalk I clawed back with a
hammer. I also added new sentences and
phrasings, having entered them as sensations

they carried. Palliative care need not be for a
mortal illness. The letter on the table makes an
echo,

one of many in the mountains.

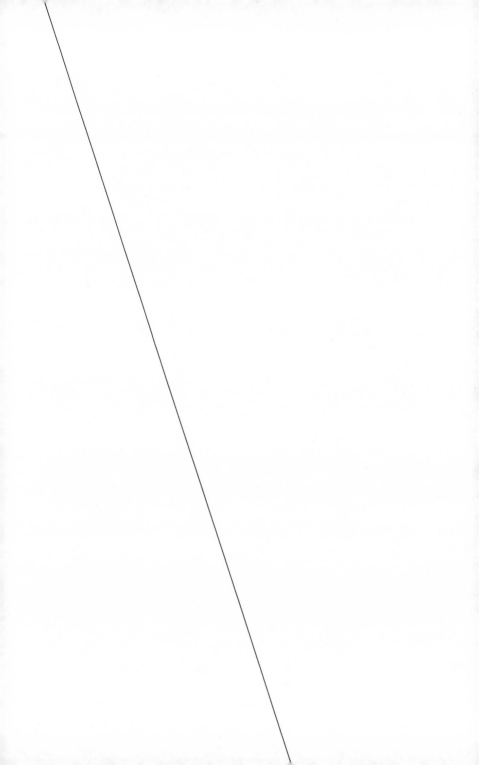

Acknowledgments

The writing practices that gave rise to this book were often shared with and written in the company of my students at Carthage College, to whom I am grateful.

My thanks to the Young Shakespeare Players and its founder, Richard DiPrima, for allowing me to experience Shakespeare's plays deeply and intimately.

I also offer special thanks for their friendship, conversation, writing, and making to: Maria Carrig, Kim Greene, Kate Greenstreet, Andy Gricevich, Alyson Kiesel, Bethany Kanter, Thomas Mowe, Daisy Rosenstock, and Chuck Stebelton. And to Joshua Beckman, for the walks and talks and most generous readings of this writing.

Many thanks to editors who published portions of this book: *Columbia Poetry Review*, from "TiP TOE SOT"; *Unearthed*, from "TiP TOE SOT"; *Tammy*, from "TiP TOE SOT."

Finally, I feel immense gratitude to Lisa Fishman, Lewis Freedman, Jordan Dunn, Max Greenstreet, and James Fishman-Morren, who offered and offer "kinship of place, time, mundanity in the continuous onrushing imagined joy."